CAREERS IN COMPUTER TECHNOLOGY™

CAREERS IN
Electronic
Publishing

PETER RYAN

ROSEN
PUBLISHING

NEW YORK

Published in 2014 by The Rosen Publishing Group, Inc.
29 East 21st Street, New York, NY 10010

First Edition

Library of Congress Cataloging-in-Publication Data

Ryan, Peter K.
Careers in electronic publishing/Peter Ryan.—First edition.
    pages cm.—(Careers in computer technology)
Includes bibliographical references and index.
ISBN 978-1-4488-9590-8
1. Electronic publishing—Vocational guidance—Juvenile literature.
2. Publishers and publishing—Vocational guidance—Juvenile literature.
I. Title.
Z286.E43R93 2014
070.5'73—dc23

                                                        2012045604

Manufactured in the United States of America

CPSIA Compliance Information: Batch #S13YA: For further information, contact Rosen Publishing, New York, New York, at
1-800-237-9932.

0100010010101101110101011010101010011001001011001001010101011010101010100100101010101

Contents

The publishing industry has been in existence for hundreds of years. Historically the main output in the industry has been printed books, magazines, and newspapers. However, the past two decades have changed the entire nature of the publishing business, caused almost entirely by the explosion of advances in computer technology and the Internet.

In the past, the typical career path for someone in the publishing business would revolve around paper-based reading, editing, layout, print staging, printing presses, and physical distribution. Today, a large percentage of the products created in the publishing industry are digital. Modern readers use computers, cell phones, tablets, and other devices to access their reading material, along with traditionally printed books.

In order to deliver content to readers across all their devices and in all the formats and languages that readers want, publishers have evolved

Tablets are fast becoming one of the most popular devices on which readers can access published content such as books and magazines.

very quickly into high-tech organizations with huge information technology requirements. As a result of this evolution, the careers and jobs in the publishing industry have changed dramatically.

The following information will cover how to prepare for a career in publishing, including educational requirements, such as an undergraduate college degree. It will also describe the role, skill requirements, and daily expectations of editors, production editors, writers, and designers.

The future of the publishing industry is hard to predict, but it is certain that it will continue to change. A career in publishing is most definitely going to be one that requires cutting-edge computer and software skills, along with the ability to identify new ways of reaching readers. The publishing industry needs bright young minds to help define the future of the industry.

CHAPTER 1

Education and Preparation

The path to a career in electronic publishing requires dedication, hard work, and a strong love of creative media. Because of the rapid adoption of technology in the industry, a career in publishing also requires strong computer skills.

At the most basic level, a career in publishing requires very strong skills in reading, writing, communications, and teamwork. It is critical that students develop good study skills and habits in order to prepare themselves for the rigor and discipline required to successfully complete an undergraduate program.

Students interested in electronic publishing should read as much as possible at all times. Learning to critically evaluate writing comes only after a lot of reading. Students should read novels, textbooks, newspapers, magazines, and Web content in order to develop strong comprehension and analysis skills. A career in publishing revolves around the written word, so a true love of reading will only serve to strengthen career goals.

Similarly any student interested in a career in publishing should write a great deal in order to develop good writing and editing skills. Basic editing is a foundational skill set upon which any career in publishing will rely heavily. Mastering editing sets a student apart as being passionate about working with writing.

Earning a college degree is essential for those interested in working in the electronic publishing field. A bachelor of

Working with only a laptop, any student can do the work of a desktop publisher. Word processing software makes it possible for authors and editors to work from anywhere.

arts typically requires students to take core classes in art, science, history, mathematics, languages, and writing. These classes expose the student to a broad array of concepts and ideas that are important to understanding the core intellectual principles. Understanding these basic principles is key to enabling a young writer or editor to create and edit content that will capture the attention of audiences.

In many cases some positions in publishing may require more than a bachelor's degree. It may be prudent to consider earning a master's degree in the field of choice in order to gain a competitive advantage over one's peers. There are many schools that offer programs that focus specifically on the publishing field and have classes that are tailored to prepare a student for specific publishing roles and challenges. Master's degrees are much more focused than bachelor's degrees, and the student will get a much more specific education from a master's field than from a bachelor's program.

TECHNICAL SKILLS

Students should gain exposure as early as possible to software programs that are used in the publishing industry. Such software includes Microsoft Word, the Adobe Creative Suite, and the Quark Publishing Platform. These two suites have been in widespread use in the publishing industry for more than a decade. Photoshop is one of the elements of the Adobe family of products, and its use is so widespread throughout the digital photography world that "Photoshop" has earned a place as a verb in the English dictionary.

The fundamental software skills that should be pursued are image manipulation, editing, layout, and Web site publishing

Sophisticated publishing and layout software often requires higher-end computer hardware.

and blogging. These skills are at the core of desktop publishing and are the cornerstone of modern publishing.

Students should learn basic photography skills, including composition, lighting, color, and capture techniques. They

should also learn how to manipulate digital photographs using software tools that include Photoshop, as well as online photo-editing software such as that offered by Google. In addition, students should practice how to shoot and edit digital video as well as how to publish that video content online.

Students need to learn the difference between shooting rough personal work on a smartphone and expert professional-grade work captured with high-end specialized equipment. Most schools have an audio-visual club or department that will be able to provide students access to high-quality equipment. Students should be sure to join those clubs and learn how to work with that specialized equipment.

COMPUTER SKILLS

Students should learn how to work with computer file systems, understand file formats, and read and write basic software coding. Particular emphasis should be placed on developing an understanding of XML (extensible markup language), which is at the core of most content management systems used by electronic publishers.

Other programming languages that a student should begin to master during their high school years are hypertext markup language (HTML) and cascading style sheets (CSS). Most Web sites are created using HTML and CSS. These languages are standard and universally applicable to almost any

Web site in any country. Even if a student doesn't intend to be a computer programmer, HTML and CSS should be part of the skill set that an aspiring writer or editor develops to get an understanding of how words are displayed on screen.

Those students who intend to focus on more technically sophisticated computer operations should begin to learn as much about computer programming as early as possible. Learning the basics about programming languages such as Java and C++ will not only serve anyone interested in digital publishing well, but it will also empower them for career flexibility for their entire professional lives.

If creative, focused students can develop technical skills during their high school years, they will be much better prepared for the demands of college and professional work in publishing than their peers. Being better prepared in the professional world translates to earning better pay, earning better positions in a company, and being able to work on the best projects available.

BUSINESS SKILLS

Business skills are a necessity for anyone interested in the field of publishing. This is true for all areas in the industry because ultimately the goal of publishing businesses is profit. Without profit, publishers will go out of business, thus eliminating jobs and salaries. Some career paths in publishing have higher financial skill requirements than others. Nonetheless all roles in publishing require at least a basic understanding of business.

In order to gain business skills while in high school, it is critical that students pursue any clubs that are business

WORD PROCESSING

Word processors are software tools used to craft written content. There are many different types of word processors made by different software companies. There are word processors for specific tasks, such as writing manuscripts, screenplays, software code, and general correspondence. Regardless of your role in the publishing industry, you will almost certainly use word processing software nearly every day.

The most popular word processing software is Microsoft Word, which produces documents that end with the .doc software extension. The .doc format is the global standard for general-purpose word processing and just about every word processing software program in the marketplace can open, edit, and save documents in the .doc format. There are many other companies that make word processing software that is similar to Microsoft Word, and generally these programs all behave in a similar fashion.

A student should become familiar and comfortable using Microsoft Word as soon as possible. This will ensure that when beginning studies at college, he or she will be able to meet the heavy writing requirement demanded. Furthermore, any student considering a career in publishing should be skilled in word processing by the time he or she graduates from college.

Microsoft Word can be a bit expensive, but there are many free alternatives that a student can download to learn with. OpenOffice is one software platform that is free, legitimate, and almost identical to Word.

oriented, seek to work in fund-raising activities such as bake sales and charity drives, and participate in running a club that involves managing a budget. Students should try to find jobs outside of school that will give them exposure to business principals. They should also be seeking internships for their summer vacations in order to develop skills and connections.

Students should specifically understand the concepts of profit and loss within a business. In addition, students should learn basic budgeting skills, specifically how to keep track of a budget using Microsoft Excel or similar spreadsheet software such as Google Docs.

COMMUNICATION SKILLS

Learning how to write and speak articulately and effectively is a must for anyone seeking a professional career. Communicating

Learning effective communication skills is very important to a successful career in publishing. Public speaking is one of the best ways to develop confidence in a team setting.

clearly and successfully via social media is a must for anyone who desires a job in publishing. Social media skills are not generally taught at the high school level, so it is incumbent on students to seek an internship or employment opportunity where they can learn those skills.

Marketers in the publishing industry are masters of social media; they use it daily to communicate with customers and to learn about markets. Many students use Facebook every day but may not possess the skills to harness the power of social media to achieve business objectives.

Students should learn how to use every social media platform available and remain abreast of changes and trends that are relevant. If a new platform emerges, the student should take the time to learn about it and how to use it. Students should strive to master one or two platforms. Having a deep knowledge of a specific platform will give students an advantage in the future.

CHAPTER 2

Basic Concepts in Electronic Publishing

One of the biggest challenges facing publishers is managing the production process of written content to keep costs in control. A single book project may require the production team to create ten digital versions of the same book in order to be able to sell them on all of the popular e-reader platforms in the marketplace.

PRODUCTION

Production is the process of converting written content into a publishable format. In order to achieve profitability in the face of evolving consumer trends, publishers have embraced technology to reduce the workflow to the fewest steps allowing the most variety in output. "Workflow" is the term used to describe the process for moving a project through the production cycle.

A workflow can be the process an editor uses to receive new written material, read and edit that material, mark that material for revision, send the material back for revision, and then await the return of the revised content. A workflow for a layout editor can be to receive photo content and process it for application on a given page, mark the content with XML and metadata, and then submit it to a content management system (CMS).

Adding to the complexity of the production process is the translation of the work into multiple languages for international distribution. This requires that the book be read and translated by people who understand the subtleties and nuances of local languages to avoid confusing the reader. A phrase in one language may not make sense when translated literally into another language, requiring translators to make edits to account for these differences.

DISTRIBUTION

Bookstores and digital storefronts are called distributors; they distribute books to the end customer. Once a project has finished the production phase it enters distribution. A

The Amazon Kindle was a major step forward in the arena of digital distribution of written content. With the Kindle, Amazon had captured the content, the method of distribution, and the platform for reading.

publishing house may produce a successful book, but e-book manufacturers and bookstore chains are responsible for selling books to the general public.

Publishers work with the content distributors to sell the final product. The publisher gets access to the millions of users who buy the e-book on their device, and the e-book maker gets a cut of the sale from enabling the publisher to sell it. These relationships create what are called distribution channels, channels that allow for products to efficiently reach consumers.

E-book hardware manufacturers such as Apple (iPad) and Amazon (Kindle) have created both the devices that readers purchase and the digital marketplaces where readers purchase content. These combinations of hardware, software, and service delivery are called content platforms. Content platforms enable many readers to be reached quickly and efficiently by the publishers who create the content.

COPYRIGHT AND PIRACY

With the ease of distribution of electronic content comes the risk of piracy. Because a small digital file can be shared across the Internet with almost no cost or barriers, it is a real challenge for publishers to protect the copyrighted works they produce. Publishers have formed coalitions to create standardized file formats and encryption methods to protect the digital content they create from being illegally duplicated or redistributed. One method of protecting content is digital rights management, or DRM. DRM uses a variety of software tools to ensure that if someone has not paid for content, it cannot be viewed.

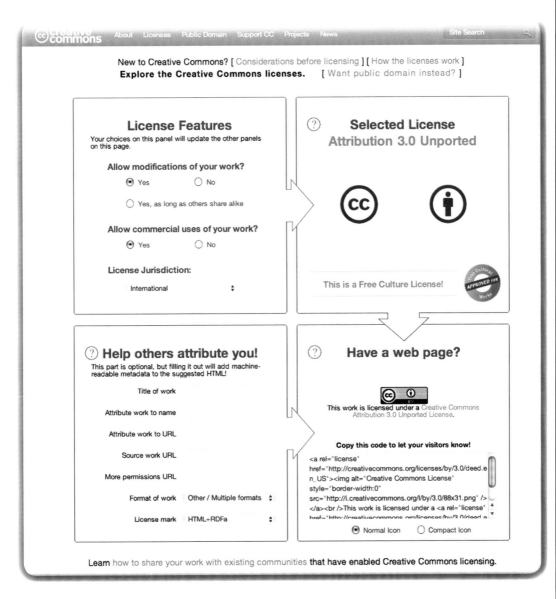

The formation of the creative commons licensing guidelines has enabled content creators to protect their work while providing limited reuse of that content for educators and other authorized users.

In addition to combating piracy with DRM, publishers have chosen to work with partners such as Apple and Amazon to embed copyright protection in the overall design of their products and platforms. The iPad and the Kindle have made purchasing digital content cheap and easy. The consumer searches in a secure digital store for content and purchases it using a stored credit card. The content downloads automatically and then is immediately available in the appropriate app for consumption. This combination of ease of use and low price makes the effort and time required for pirating content a losing proposition.

Despite the best efforts of the publishing industry and the technology industry to protect the copyrighted content

TOUCH-TYPING

One skill that generally goes unrecognized when discussing preparation for a college degree or a professional career is typing. The art of typing is now more important than ever before. Anyone who has an interest in a career in publishing should take formal typing training as part of his or her preparation for graduation from high school.

The ability to type quickly and accurately without looking at the keyboard is a skill that will be used every day in the publishing industry. Touch-typing skills will greatly improve the productivity and efficiency of an aspiring editor or writer. Those who don't learn to touch-type and use the "hunt and peck" method of looking at the keys as they type are at best able to get up to about thirty-five words per minute typing. Those who are trained in touch-typing average about fifty words per minute, and those who train and practice extensively are able to get their speed above one hundred words per minute.

of authors, piracy still exists, and likely will always exist. With each new advance made by law-abiding companies to curb piracy, a new way to steal will be discovered. This creates a perpetual challenge for the publishing industry and creates a constant cost that must be attached to each product created.

MARKETING AND ADVERTISING

Two very important parts of publishing are marketing and advertising. Marketing is the study of consumer behavior to try to determine what products would be most appealing, and thus most likely to sell. Marketing experts study consumers to learn what they like and dislike, how they behave, and how much money they typically spend on products in order to better understand what products and product attributes would be most appealing to customers.

In electronic publishing, market researchers will study the kinds of digital products that people buy and the people who buy them. For example, if a marketing executive at Marvel Comics wants to know what comic books may be popular next year, she will study what comic books people are buying today, across a range of ages, locations, sexes, and any other bits of data that can be found. This research can help the company understand who their customers are and what they like so that they can make a product the customer would be likely to purchase.

Advertising is the practice of placing messages in front of customers about upcoming and current products. Advertisers tell the public about products that they should purchase using a wide variety of delivery mechanisms to reach their targeted

Marketing teams create and execute a marketing plan that can turn a book into a major success.

audience. We are all familiar with advertising because we are surrounded by advertisements every day.

Though we all know what advertising is, the science of advertising is often overlooked. Advertisers pay close attention to market trends and create ads that are tailored to maximum effect for target groups.

BUSINESS MODEL

Within the electronic publishing universe, there are many different models that publishers use to charge their customers for content. Traditionally publishers would sell books to

The iPad has provided publishers with a very large pool of potential readers through its storefront. This ease of purchasing books increases sales, which benefits both Apple and publishers.

bookstores, which would then sell books to readers. Printing books required substantial cash investment, and bookstores required lots of space to store inventory.

In the new era of digital content, there is no inventory and there are no printing costs. The costs in electronic publishing are related to the packaging of content in as many forms possible. These costs are not as great as printing and inventory costs in the old model, but the price per unit sold is also lower in digital form. The result is that the profitability is about the same and in some cases is even lower for electronic content.

The loss of profitability has incited publishers to experiment with alternative methods for selling content. Some have tried selling content through a subscription model whereby the consumer purchases access to a pool of content and gets to choose a certain number of items for download. Others have tried breaking large pieces of content into smaller ones and selling the small pieces as episodes or chapters of content, charging slightly more for all the chapters individually than the price of the entire book.

Experimentation in business models will continue for a long time to come because selling digital content is entirely new. Publishers will persist in seeking innovative ways to sell content and engage with customers.

CHAPTER 3

Generally speaking, an editor is responsible for the overall management of a publishing project and has the responsibility to oversee anyone involved in a project, to manage the profit and loss, and to ensure that everyone on the team has all the resources required to complete their work.

Editors are the first to receive new content from authors, and they are the first to determine if the content merits publication. In order to be able to discern the projects that are good enough to receive a green light to move forward from those that aren't, an editor must be well versed in a particular field or genre. Most editors specialize in a particular field or genre. Because editors specialize, they develop a unique understanding of the market for their field or genre and are able to better predict what may sell.

Editors are constantly looking for new talent to produce the next big project. They are also constantly watching the marketplace to understand what kinds of trends are shaping the decisions of consumers. Editors are essential to the continued growth of publishing companies.

When an editor finds a new prospective author, they will request a sample of work or a proposal for a project in order to determine if the author's work and capability will merit a successful, profitable plan. One of the first things that an editor will try to determine is if the author's project fits within the larger scope of work that the publishing firm is working on.

Editors use many software applications to edit text. This is true across most editorial roles, so it is critical that anyone looking for an editorial career develop strong computer skills.

It is important to understand that publishing companies have many projects being developed at any given time. Publishing companies view projects in process as pieces of a larger portfolio of work. The portfolio will be designed

to achieve certain marketplace and financial goals. A large publishing company will look ahead and try to determine what kinds of projects will likely be successful. They use their collective knowledge of the current marketplace and their understanding of specific fields and genres to create project goals and targets to work toward. Once the inventory of goals is created, it is then the responsibility of the editors to find new content to fill their publishing "list."

DIFFERENT KINDS OF EDITORS

It is important to note that there are many different kinds of editors across the world of publishing. There are even different names for different editorial roles within different areas of publishing. For instance, editors in the newspaper industry have similar titles to editors working in the traditional book publishing industry, but their roles are substantially different. The emphasis of this book is traditional publishing, and what follows is a generalization of editorial roles that may be commonly found across book publishers.

ACQUISITIONS EDITOR

Acquisitions editors are responsible for bringing new content to a publishing house. They work with literary agents and authors and do a lot of scouting to find new writers who may produce work that will sell well for the publisher.

An acquisitions editor will receive many manuscript submissions from many different sources. Some authors will

Attention to detail is a critical skill that any editor must possess. Reviewing manuscript drafts on paper can be an important part of the editing process because it helps the editor understand how the final printed product will look and feel.

submit their work directly to an acquisitions editor. Some authors will retain the help of an agent, who will submit manuscripts to acquisitions editors on their behalf. In either case acquisitions editors receive a lot of manuscripts, and most of them will not be accepted for publication.

In order for acquisitions editors to manage the volume of manuscripts received, they will employ assistant editors and manuscript readers. The assistants and readers will read incoming manuscripts and either accept a manuscript that they feel the acquisitions editor would want to pursue, or they reject it. Assistants and readers generally know what the goals and tastes of the acquisitions editor are and will pick manuscripts that they know the acquisitions editor would like to consider publishing.

After a manuscript has been read and accepted for further consideration by an assistant editor or a reader, it ends up in the hands of the acquisitions editor. The acquisition editor will evaluate the manuscript on many levels. Will the manuscript fit within the goals of the publisher? Will the manuscript be marketable? Will the manuscript, if published, conflict with any other projects being developed by the publisher? Will the manuscript sell?

Once an author's manuscript has been accepted and approved by the acquisitions editor, the author and the editor will work very closely on any changes and adjustments to the book. The acquisitions editor will be the primary point of contact for the author and will serve as the author's advocate throughout the duration of the project.

A key role the acquisitions editor plays is as a liaison between the author and the publishing company. The acquisitions editor works with many parts of the publishing firm. He or she will work with the legal team to draft contracts, with the finance department to ensure payments are made to the author, with the marketing team to advertise the book, and with the production team to ensure that it is ready for printing and distribution.

Acquisitions editors must have many skills to accomplish their jobs. They must also have very strong math and finance skills to ensure that projects are properly forecast and budgeted. They must be able to manipulate complex spreadsheets and easily navigate word processing software to make

TRACKING CHANGES

When working in team environments, individuals are often required to share word processing documents and to draft, edit, and approve content collaboratively. When two or more people are collaborating on the same document, it can be very difficult to find where in a document changes or additions have been made. In order to make collaboration easier most writers and editors will use "track changes" when working on documents.

Most word processing software has a special feature called "track changes," which when activated keeps records, which are color coded by editor, of all changes that are made to a document. If two or more people are collaborating on the same document, each change that each person makes will be added to the document with a unique color that makes it easy to find.

sure that editing is properly documented and that versions of the manuscript are kept in proper order.

DEVELOPMENTAL EDITOR

A developmental editor's role is similar to that of an acquisitions editor. He or she is also responsible for bringing new projects to life for a publisher. However, unlike an acquisitions editor, developmental editors may also create concept plans and go about finding authors and content creators to satisfy development plans.

Developmental editors are usually given the task of building a portfolio of books for a given time period with a set of

Developmental editors work with teams of other editors, designers, and marketers on their projects. They have to bring together the many professionals working on the manuscript to make it a cohesive finished book.

specific requirements. For example, a publisher may want to produce a series of books on a very relevant topic currently in the news and may want the books to be available in the market within a short period of time. They will usually have a set budget and financial objective to accomplish.

Though the charter of the developmental editor is substantially different from that of the acquisitions editor, their day-to-day roles can be very similar. They spend a lot of their time reading manuscripts, approving author contracts, communicating with authors, shepherding projects from concept to production, and keeping track of finances and budgets.

COPY EDITOR

A copy editor is responsible for reading manuscripts once they have been substantially completed and checking for any grammatical errors or problems that should be corrected. Copy editors look at issues such as writing style and word choice to determine whether changes should be made to enhance the quality of a manuscript.

It is the job of the copy editor to ensure that a manuscript is written in a way that adheres to the overall guidelines of a given project. They seek words that are not appropriate for the targeted reader and replace them with words that will be easily understood or that will fit better. They seek grammatical errors and adjust them where needed. They also look for oddly phrased sentences and paragraphs and mark the manuscript for revision by the author.

Another important role of the copy editor may be to ensure that the content in a manuscript is accurate and factual. If a manuscript were to contain inaccuracies or elements that in any way defamed or harmed the reputation of a person, company or other entity, it could open doors for legal troubles and the potential for lawsuits.

PROOFREADER

The job of the proofreader in the digital era has dramatically changed. In the past, proofreaders were responsible for looking for typographic errors and problems with the physical

Copy editors use a standardized notation system to edit manuscripts. This standard system allows anyone else on the publication team to understand the copy editor's changes.

layout of pages. This was critical because once a book went to print, it would be very costly to reprint pages and impossible to change once a book had been bound.

Today a proofreader still checks copy for layout and typographical issues. The biggest difference is that proofreaders are able to use software to help them scan many manuscripts for any issues very rapidly. This is especially true of typographical errors; spell-checking software helps to automate the search for typos in books. However, there does need to be a person who scans a book's layout and the final preprint manuscript to ensure it is error-free and ready for publication.

Students should experiment with track changes to become familiar with the conceptual use of the tools and to become comfortable with the actual use and mechanics of the feature.

The role of a production editor is to manage and coordinate book projects through the production process to ensure that they are completed and ready to print on time and within budget. A production editor has an attentive eye for detail, can manage a team of people, can manage a budget, runs a tight schedule, and works closely with writers and designers to integrate all aspects of a project into a professional finished product.

Production editors are the center of communication for most publishing projects once they've begun. The editor gathers all the work from anyone contributing to a project, including writers, artists, fact checkers, proofreaders, editing staff, the legal department, marketing, and finance. The production editor is the person in the middle of it all making sure that the project gets completed on time and on budget.

CONTENT PRODUCTION

The production editor is responsible for working with authors and artists to make sure that the materials delivered for production arrive on time and are quickly and thoroughly reviewed through a rigorous editing process. The editors' job is to find problems in any given work and to ensure those problems are corrected.

Once content has been formally edited and approved for production, it will pass hands from the author and artist to

Production editors use layout and image editing software to give a book a professional look and feel.

the design and layout teams. Designers will create packaging and graphics for the manuscript. Art and writing will be integrated into a single package and laid out digitally to ensure that the content flows properly when viewed start to finish. The production editor will coordinate the efforts of the graphics teams and the layout teams to ensure that the product is moving on schedule and if there are any issues ensuring that they are resolved quickly.

Production editors use a wide variety of tools to accomplish their jobs. Project management software that tracks a book project from start to finish is essential to ensure that every project moves through the production process in a timely fashion. Communication tools are used to guarantee that every member of the production team gets the materials needed at the right time. Financial spreadsheets are used to keep close track of costs as the project is produced and to make certain that the project is completed within the set budget.

USING DESKTOP PUBLISHING SOFTWARE

In most cases authors will submit manuscripts as Microsoft Word documents. The raw manuscript will be formatted to fit the conventions that the word processing software applies while the author writes, and that formatting will need to be altered for production.

A production editor must make sure that the fonts, layout, line spacing, margins, footnotes, and bibliography are all consistent with the publisher's requirements. This is no small

PROJECT MANAGEMENT SOFTWARE

Project management software is designed to provide project managers and project contributors with a shared timeline and framework to guide and track the scheduling and fulfillment of a project. In larger teams where many people contribute to a team effort, it is often the case that different people contribute at different times. It is also the case that in some projects some people cannot contribute to a project until some portion is already completed. Keeping track of what has been done on a project, by whom, and what the next phase of a project is can be very difficult. Project management software keeps all the information consolidated and presented in a graphical format.

Anyone interested in an editorial position should get access to and practice using project management software. Because project management can be complicated, the software that is used can also be very complex. The most commonly used project management software today is Microsoft Project, but there are many other software alternatives available, such as FileMaker.

There are many certifications available to prove competency using various project management software. There is also a professional designation that can be attained, a project management professional, or PMP. Earning a PMP certification requires taking training courses, gaining real-life experience in project management, and passing a challenging exam. The Project Management Institute, an internationally recognized body, offers the PMP designation. Earning a PMP certification would greatly prepare an editor for the challenges they will certainly face.

task, and the best way to accomplish this is by using desktop publishing software. The editor will convert the author's manuscript into a format that is usable by the publishing software. This is usually a process that is built into the software and is typically referred to as an importation process. Production editors will then import the Word document into software, such as Adobe InDesign, that lays the text into e-book format.

Once the manuscript is imported to the publishing software, it can be very easily manipulated and shared. Desktop publishing software provides tools that allow the editor to add graphics, art, custom pagination, detailed layout, and much more. Publishing software also allows for many members of the production team to collaborate on the same content simultaneously and tracks the changes that are made along with comments from each contributor. The end result is a finished book in digital format that is fit for digital publishing.

USING A CONTENT MANAGEMENT SYSTEM

To ensure that projects are produced as efficiently as possible, it is necessary for projects to be assembled into a content management system (CMS) with proper coding, tagging, metadata, and formatting. It is the role of the production editor to ensure that once a project has begun, all content is added to the CMS properly. Once the content is added to the CMS, the production editor will turn to design teams to create "skins" for the project so that each version of a project will look nearly identical despite the electronic platform the consumer uses to purchase and view the content.

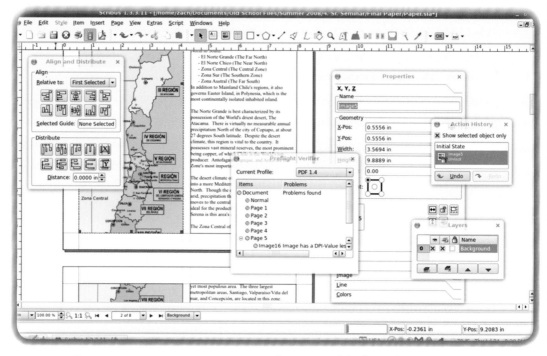

Content management systems make it possible for editors to store text, art, graphics, and other parts of a book in a database format. This database format allows for the easy retrieval of the content by others during and after the production is complete.

Using a CMS dramatically improves the overall performance and efficiency of a production team because it gives visibility to all aspects of current and past projects to anyone on the publisher's staff. It shortens the workload for creating alternate editions of the same book. It makes the process of producing alternate media versions of a book very simple. CMS tools are essential to the success of a publisher today.

PROOFREADING AND REVIEW

One major function that a production editor plays is that of proof-reader and fact checker. If the production editor finds any errors in the project work (grammatical mistakes, spelling errors, odd language structure, missing words, or sentence fragments), it is his or her job to get writers or editors to correct them.

It is also the role of the production editor to ensure that art is put in the proper places. Art, including photos and graphics, must be checked to ensure that it is inserted in the proper place and is properly cited in the project.

CATALOGING

In every published book, you will find an ISBN number. ISBN stands for International Standard Book Number. This is a thirteen-digit number that is assigned to commercially pub-lished books to identify and officially record them within a standardized framework.

ISBNs are used by bookstores and libraries to accurately identify books and to make the process of ordering books from publishers simple. Each book published receives a unique ISBN, which is stored in an ISBN database. Typically the production editor is the person responsible for attach-ing an ISBN to a book. To do this, the production editor must understand how the ISBN system works and be able to manipulate the in-house database of available ISBNs that the publisher has available. Once the ISBN is assigned to the book, it must be reported to the ISBN agency in each country where the book will be digitally published and sold.

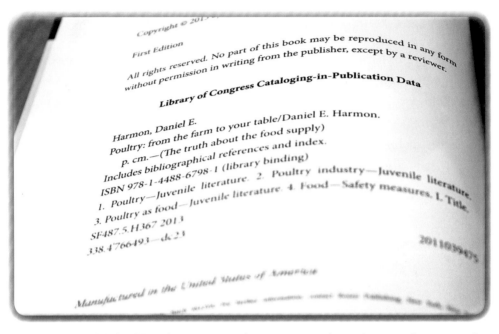

Every published book is assigned an ISBN and cataloging data issued by the Library of Congress. This information is usually available on the copyright page of a book.

MULTITASKING

The most challenging aspect of the production editor's job is managing all the previously mentioned tasks across multiple projects simultaneously. The role of production editors is critical. They are the people who most directly ensure that a book is produced in a timely fashion. If they falter, an entire project can fail.

The work of a writer in electronic publishing is to produce quality written content on time and within the scope of the project. Some writers will work under an arrangement called work for hire and create content that is requested on a particular topic. Other writers will create their own work based on their own interest. In either case, the writer's role is to create the words that draw the reader to the page.

Writers can have various talents within writing, but most will specialize in a certain field of writing. There are novelists, historical writers, biographers, science writers, technical writers, and many more. There are some writers who are able to write across the various disciplines: they are extremely talented and somewhat rare. Most writers tend to stick to a specific style of writing.

In addition to having the ability to engage readers with their writing style, writers must also understand the topics on which they write. The writer is the primary researcher of topics and in some cases will employ researchers to help prepare for the writing of the book. Some writers may even hire research assistants to help learn about all kinds of interesting subjects, with the intention of accurately employing that information in their writing. Good writers take the time to learn the subjects they write about and usually will develop a mastery of a topic.

Bob Woodward is one of the most famous journalists of his time. In addition to being a pioneering newspaperman, he is also a successful nonfiction author.

FIELDS OF WRITING

It is very important to understand that there are many different types of writer and writing styles in the world of digital publishing. There are newspaper journalists, magazine writers, writers for professional publications, science writers, and many more. Each discipline requires a different set of writing skills and styles. However, despite there being many types of writing roles there are definitive writing skills that all writers draw on.

Writing skills are learned and mastered only with constant practice. It is important for anyone looking for a career in

WRITING STYLE GUIDES

In the United States there are two dominant writing guides that almost all publishers follow: *The Chicago Manual of Style* and the *MLA Style Manual*. Journalists and newspapers, however, follow *The Associated Press Stylebook* or the newspaper's own in-house style guide.

The Chicago Manual of Style is published by the University of Chicago Press and has been in publication since 1906. The *MLA Style Manual* is published by the Modern Language Association and was first published in 1985.

These two manuals of style are indispensible tools for anyone working in the publishing industry. These manuals set out writing guidelines and structural conventions that are used by nearly all publishers. The manuals give guidelines such as how to construct a citation in a bibliography, how a block quote should be formatted, and how to use punctuation, such as quotation marks. These manuals provide a set of guides that standardize the practice of writing so that everyone who reads and writes had a common set of rules to follow.

Any student who is considering a career in publishing should spend time learning both manuals and should begin adopting the guidelines. In addition, most colleges and universities require students to follow one of the style manuals, so the sooner students learn proper style the better.

writing to practice writing every day and to write for many different kinds of projects. While in high school, there are always homework assignments that must be written, but in order to excel as a writer the student must go beyond the minimum.

The school newspaper is a great place to experience the challenge of mass publication of a student's work. The school yearbook is also a great place to get experience writing.

No matter what kind of writing field a writer eventually works within, he or she will likely need to have experience publishing online. Gaining knowledge by publishing early work on Web sites and blogs is critical. Students should learn how to use blogging tools to publish their work and become comfortable with having their work exposed to comment and criticism.

JOURNALISM, NEWSPAPERS, AND MAGAZINES

Journalism generally refers to the reporting of current events via newspapers and magazines. Journalists are trained to research facts and to write without any bias toward one side of an argument or a political agenda.

It is important to note that both the newspaper and magazine industries are in states of rapid transformation from print to digital businesses. It was less than a decade ago that the circulation of newspapers was greater in print than online. Today "newspaper" is a term loosely describing an organization that does news reporting across multiple media, including print and the Internet. The *New York Times* is the clearest example of this transformation; It is more of a content management company than a traditional newspaper company today.

Similarly, the world of TV and radio news has also undergone a radical transformation, and the content they distribute is now evenly spread across the Internet, television, and other

Journalism involves not only writing but also reporting. This involves finding stories and gathering facts, often on strict deadlines.

WRITING SCHEDULES

Some of the most famous and celebrated authors will write only a few hundred words a day. This sounds strange when you consider that authors like Stephen King can sometimes produce two or even three books a year. How would it be possible to produce so much content by writing only a few hundred words a day?

Good writers know that the volume of work produced is not nearly as important as the quality of work produced. Rather than trying to write whole chapters or entire sections of books in marathon writing sessions, professional authors will usually create scheduled and regular writing hours that begin and end within a set amount of time. This limitation of the amount of writing time per day prevents authors from burning out or from growing bored. It also helps writers to stay connected with their work by revisiting it each day.

There are some writers who can write in a marathon fashion and complete an entire book within a month. But this is a rare gift, and often not possible by most. Professional writers who earn their living by writing know that the best way to go forward is to work slowly and steadily, to give themselves time off from writing, and to protect themselves from boredom and writer's block.

media. The cause for this transformation is the growth and accessibility of the Internet, which created entirely new formats for content distribution.

NOVELISTS

Novelists are writers whose work is typically focused on book-length works of fiction. A novel will generally be hundreds of pages in length. Novelists use long-form narrative to deliver a rich and detailed body of work to the reader. Novelists are most typically published in book and e-book format.

The e-book format is attractive to publishers because the cost of distributing e-books is much lower than for physical books. The printing, distribution, and shelving of books is a very expensive process. The profitability of e-books is much greater than that of print books despite the large commission charged by e-book platforms such as the iPad or Kindle.

BLOGS AND WEB SITES

Blogs and Web sites present one of the greatest challenges the publishing business has experienced. The cost to publish a blog is nearly zero, and it is possible for anyone to create one with minimal effort. This is arguably the first time that anyone has been able to publish without having to navigate the challenges of the traditional publishing industry.

Professional blogs and Web sites face the challenge of having to create content that is compelling, of high quality, visible, and timely. There are thousands of blogs, many of which are covering the same topics. In order to really stand out among the group, the work must be exceptional. Preparation for working as a blogger or Web site writer requires years of writing to develop the tools and style to capture and keep an audience.

Bloggers are also always competing to be the first to report on a topic and the exclusive source of information on a topic. To this end it is critical that bloggers have solid research and investigatory training.

Writing for Web sites and blogs, such as Rx for Healthcare (http://www.rxforhealth.typepad.com), sometimes requires special skill sets, including a basic knowledge of HTML and other Web programming languages.

SALARY VERSUS FREELANCE VERSUS SUPERSTAR

Although it is the dream of most writers to be successful top-tier authors whose names are instantly recognizable by any reader, making a living off of writing is challenging. The majority of writers are not well known and in many cases may not ever achieve any degree of notoriety or brand-name recognition. Most writers are motivated by the mere love of writing itself.

Despite the odds against superstardom for most authors, writing can be a full-time profession for many people. There are people who are full-time staff writers whose job is to create content at a publishing house and who are paid to consistently produce. There are freelance writers who are hired as outside contractors to write on specific topics for a variety of publishers. There are also name-brand authors such as James Patterson and J. K. Rowling who have achieved enormous success. Though there are many freelance writers and very few superstar authors, there is a very wide field of opportunity and employment in the middle.

CHAPTER 6

Designer

In the world of publishing, the role of the designer is becoming ever more important. Historically, design in publishing has been relegated to cover art, marketing materials, and illustration. With the digitization of content and the changing tastes of consumers, designers are now required to have a hand in almost every aspect of all projects.

Digital content has art, graphics, dynamic audio and visual elements, and video content. The designer must be part of the project from its inception to ensure that there is a uniform design style and that the aesthetic of the work is consistent with the overall goals of the publisher.

TOOLS OF THE TRADE

Most designers will work within many different formats and media to accomplish their work. All will at some point use desktop publishing tools such as Adobe Photoshop or InDesign to manipulate photographs or create new original work.

There are some cases when designers will work with physical media. Ink, pencils, paper, and other traditional art supplies are still widely used. Although the art may be created using traditional tools, it will be scanned and converted to a digital format for inclusion in the final digital product and for storage in the CMS.

GRABBING THE READER

Although it may seem unlikely, the work of the designer is often as critical to the commercial success of some titles as the advertisers and marketers. Cover art is essential for the success of books in some genres. This is particularly true in fantasy, science fiction, and some children's books.

Cover art is an artist's interpretation of the general feeling, tone, and gist of a book. An artist will need to read the book in question and then work with both the author and editor to capture as much detail about the author's intentions in

Depending on the type of book, the look of a book is sometimes as important as the text. Graphic designers must work hard to express visually a book's subject matter.

PHOTOSHOP AND INDESIGN

Did you know that the most widely used photo editing and manipulation tool in use today is Adobe Photoshop? Photoshop was first developed and sold in 1990 and is now in its thirteenth major iteration, or version. Photoshop is such a widely used product that it has become synonymous with the process of manipulating digital photos.

Photoshop is an indispensible tool for designers in the publishing industry. Designers use it to crop, touch-up, enhance, and alter photos. Possessing strong Photoshop skills is essential for anyone considering a role as a designer in the publishing industry.

Adobe InDesign is one of the most widely used desktop publishing tools. InDesign makes it possible for designers to create custom layouts, add pictures, manage typography, and much more. InDesign is part of the Adobe Creative Suite, commonly referred to as Adobe CS.

Adobe InDesign is a very powerful tool and also a very complex one. Adobe has created a training and certification program for design professionals. The InDesign certification is part of a larger certification process to be an Adobe Certified Expert (ACE). Anyone who earns the ACE has a mastery of most, if not all, of the Adobe suite of products and is well prepared to use Adobe tools in the publishing industry.

Most authors will create their manuscript using word processing software like Microsoft Word. Word processors are great for giving authors the tools to write their manuscript but are insufficient for the final production process. Word processors typically will lay text out in an 8.5 inches by 11 inches (21.6 centimeters by 28 centimeters) format, standard letter size. There are many formats that books are published in, but 8.5 inches by 11 inches is not common. Using InDesign, the designer must account for changes in spacing and layout to accommodate the entirety of the manuscript into the production size of the book.

the book to establish an artistic theme and goal for the cover. In some cases artists may be asked to create multiple concepts for the cover art to give the editor and author a chance to choose what they feel best fits the book.

Cover art can set a book apart from its peers simply because it may be able to catch a potential reader's eye over other books. For some readers the cover art of a book may set their imagination down a particular path as they begin to read the book, so it is critical that the art be truly representative of the author's work.

LAYOUT

Layout is often taken for granted by both readers and writers. Layout is the physical composition of text on a readable surface. It can be the layout of print on a sheet of paper, or it can be the layout of rich media on a digital screen. Regardless of the medium that is being used, every published product must go through a layout process.

Layout incorporates many different elements, including font choice, word spacing, line height, paragraph indentation, paragraph spacing, and more. All of the choices that a designer makes while laying a book out will determine the overall aesthetic appeal of the finished product. A designer can enhance the work of an author through the effective use of layout.

AESTHETIC COORDINATION

In order for a book to feel like a polished product, it must have a consistent design. The fonts must all be coordinated, the colors must be from the same palette, the artistic elements must complement each other, and so on. There are many people who participate in the artistic creation of all the design elements that go into a book. The person who is responsible for overseeing the coordination of those efforts is the designer.

A designer on a project will work closely with the acquisitions or developmental editor, the author or author's agent, and the marketing department on the overall aesthetic of the book. It is the role of the designer to tie all of the visual elements of the book into an attractive package.

Some e-readers are restrictive in terms of how much stylization or design can be applied to an e-book. It is the role of the layout editor to create a comfortable look and feel with those limited options.

The overall look and feel of a book or magazine is sometimes as important to its success as the content. People are highly sensitive to design and artistic quality, even if not fully conscious of it. Attractive products are more appealing than unattractive ones. Attraction and beauty are subjective and often not commonly shared across society. Finding beauty and appealing design is the job of the designer, to apply grace to what is essentially a manuscript.

DAY-TO-DAY OF A DESIGNER

Designers spend much of their time working with software tools to manipulate pages and art. They will participate in meetings with people from many different departments to discuss the design of projects. They will work under tight deadlines and with strict scrutiny from editors and marketers.

A designer must have excellent art skills and be well trained. A degree in art studies or some form of art application is preferable. Designers should also have a well-rounded education with plenty of study in the humanities to give them the literary background needed to thrive in the publishing industry. A designer must also be very collaborative and able to work well with others people in very stressful and demanding situations.

CHAPTER 7

Marketing and Distribution

Marketing in today's digital world requires the use of many avenues of communication, including print, Internet, television, and social media. Using multiple methods of communication requires using many forms of media. Effectively marketing a product or service also requires a consistent and uniform message across different platforms of communication.

Marketing professionals create effective messages about the products they sell and deliver those messages to a target audience. The target audience is made up of people who the marketer believes would be most likely to purchase the product. This task requires that the marketer study the trends in the marketplace to understand what people are buying. It also calls for marketers to study the marketing channels that are most effective at converting advertising into sales.

MARKETING CHANNELS

A marketing channel is a method or mode of communication used to communicate with potential customers. Facebook is one marketing channel, and television advertising is another. Facebook and television have different audiences, so the message that is communicated over Facebook may not be the same as the message communicated over television.

XML AND EPUB

Considering the many people who use e-readers and digital tablets and the huge success of digital books, it is highly advisable for someone interested in a technology-focused career in the publishing industry to learn how to read and write XML and how to work the EPUB format.

XML makes it possible for content to be rapidly manipulated and assembled into many configurations. EPUB is the most common format used for electronic books. Understanding how XML works and how it fits in with EPUB is a skill that more and more people are learning today. Within a short amount of time it will be standard for even the lowest-level production editor to know how to code XML and to format books in EPUB.

A great way to learn these skills is to experiment with free tools available from software developers. Apple's iBooks Author is a free tool that anyone with a Mac can download and experiment with. Calibre is a free tool that anyone with a PC can use to create EPUB files. There are also many Web sites and books on the topic that can help make learning easier.

Electronic publishing software, such as Calibre, allows publishers to distribute books seamlessly across many channels, including computer screens, tablets, and smartphone apps, as illustrated in this screenshot from the Calibre Web site.

The traditional marketing channels that publishers have relied on are ads in newspapers, in magazines, on billboards, on television, on the radio, and on the Internet. Each advertising channel requires different types of advertising tools and methods and requires people with different skills to accomplish the job. TV ads are very different from print ads in newspapers, so different teams are used to create the various advertisements.

The introduction of social media has dramatically altered the landscape for marketing and advertising. Facebook and Twitter are now almost as effective, if not more so, than

Facebook and other social media sites have become critical advertising channels for publishers. Young readers learn about new books from their friends, and advertisers work hard to advertise into that social network.

traditional advertising. Social media also provides the added benefit of providing detailed data about customers and customer feedback.

ADVERTISING COMPANIES

Publishing marketing teams will usually have some amount of in-house advertising capability to create content for most advertising formats. In some cases when a special skill or capability is required, a marketing team may hire an outside firm to create an advertisement. This is especially true for TV and Web campaigns. Outside firms are usually retained if a book achieves significant success in the market, and the marketing team can easily justify the added expense of hiring outside help to create advertising content.

For most midmarket books, or those that are moderately successful but not huge hits, internal marketing resources are the only tools available to advertise the books. Social media has provided an entirely new and powerful set of tools for marketing teams to use to communicate to potential audiences about upcoming books. Rather than a single message blasted across the television or radio, marketers can create personalized and narrowly focused advertising campaigns on Facebook and Twitter. These micro-campaigns are better able to pinpoint the target audience and deliver specific messages, and cost a fraction of a traditional marketing campaign.

AUTHOR AS MARKETER

One unanticipated effect of social media is the enhancement of dialogue between the author and the audience. Historically, if readers wanted to communicate with an author, they would send a letter to the publisher, who then may or may not forward that along to the author. With social media tools, a reader can send messages directly to the author and get a response in a very short amount of time.

Many midmarket authors are very excited about the power of social media because it helps level the marketing playing field. When a book is initially accepted for publication, it is given a set marketing budget, but sometimes that budget is lower than necessary to market the book effectively. Authors who don't achieve high sales quickly won't see any additional marketing support from the publisher. Authors who do achieve rapid commercial success will get additional marketing support from publishers in the form of advertising campaigns to further accelerate sales.

Most authors are midmarket commercially, so there is always a fair amount of frustration that only the very best selling books get the majority of marketing support. Social media empowers authors to promote their own work, and the more they work at it the more likely their efforts will pay off in the form of increased sales.

SOCIAL MEDIA PROFESSIONALS

In cases where books become enormously successful, it is likely that managing social media presences across all the major social networks will become a full-time job. In those cases, publishers will hire full-time social media coordinators. Their job is to work closely with marketing to deliver consistent messages about the book to the public via social networks. It is also the responsibility of the social media professional to

Social media sites such as Twitter have become some of the best places to get the word out about upcoming publications.

moderate any negative commentary that may develop to prevent negative sentiment from growing out of control.

Social media moderators also gather feedback from readers about the content they oversee and pass that information on to the marketing teams. Authors and editors will also be given feedback from the social networks in order to help them improve or alter future work so that it will better satisfy the wants of consumers.

CHAPTER 8

Content Platforms and Technology

In order to achieve increased efficiency in publishing, content management systems have been widely adopted and used by most publishing houses. As discussed earlier, content management systems make the task of organizing, cataloging, preparing, and distributing content much faster and thus cheaper.

Using content management systems requires that publishers hire information technology specialists to deploy, manage, and maintain the CMS software and hardware. The software is comprised of client software, which is the user interface that the production teams interact with, and of server software, where the data lives and is managed. The hardware consists of networking equipment, desktop computers, and servers. Because an effective CMS is so critical to the everyday operation of publishing companies, it is essential that the hardware and software is working properly at all times. This is where IT specialists perform their role, keeping the productivity tools working.

CONTENT MANAGEMENT SYSTEMS

When a publisher goes through the process of choosing to use a CMS, they must decide between building their own in-house system from the ground up or to purchase a CMS from a vendor. The reasons behind building one instead of buying one are very complex, but ultimately it comes down to cost and goals.

The company that chooses to build its own CMS most likely has a specific publishing requirement that calls for a very customized CMS platform. Some companies may have an internally built system that was initially deployed many years ago and is now so important to the workflows of the company that switching to another would be very disruptive and costly.

The benefits of buying a prebuilt CMS platform are reduced development costs, quick deployment time, and ongoing customer support from a dedicated team of engineers. A prebuilt, ready-to-install CMS generally incorporates the tools and inherent workflow engine capability that embodies industry-wide best practices.

There are opportunities for those who possess the computer skills to support and maintain the critical operations of a CMS. Publishing teams rely on a functioning and well-maintained data management system. In the case of a CMS crash or failure all projects that rely on the CMS come to a halt until the CMS can be repaired and reinitialized.

E-BOOKS

The success of e-books requires that all publishers create e-book and electronic versions of all projects produced. This is true for books, newspapers, magazines, and trade publications. Whatever content a publisher produces must be made available in a wide variety of formats across a diverse set of devices. The most popular and recognizable e-book readers and tablets that most consumers use are the

The Nook from Barnes & Noble is just one of a handful of e-readers competing to capture the attention of book buyers.

Apple iPad, the Android Tablet, the Amazon Kindle, and the Barnes & Noble Nook.

When a publisher decides to sell its content through any of the digital platforms, it must go through an application process for each platform, each of which is owned by a different corporate entity, and thus must enter into a legal contract with each platform provider. When content is sold on a digital device, the platform provider will perform the financial transaction and collect funds from the consumer. The platform provider will then retain a portion of the transaction as a commission for the sale and will then pay the balance remaining to the publisher. The commission sizes depend on

INFORMATION TECHNOLOGY

Because of the enormous change in the way that publishers perform their work today, the role of information technology has become critical. Publishers cannot afford to have computer downtime, to lose any data, or to have any security breaches. Keeping computer systems running, healthy, and safe requires a dedicated staff of IT professionals.

In publishing, there are several distinct IT roles. System administrators manage and maintain the massive data systems that store all of the digital content that publishers create. They make sure that data is available, that it is safe, and that there will always be room to grow. There are also help desk professionals whose role is to assist publishing staff with any workstation-related problems. They make sure that everyone in the company is able to do their work on safe and healthy computers.

If you are interested in a role that is more technical in nature but are still attracted to the publishing industry, you may want to consider a role as an information technology professional in the publishing industry.

the platform company and upon the terms of the financial contract between the publisher and the platform.

There are many formats that are used for digital distribution of written or artistic work. EPUB is the most standardized format used for the distribution of written content to e-readers and tablets. EPUB formatting is usually built into the CMS as a standard output for all projects. MP3 and AAC are the most common formats for digital music, while MPEG4 and MOV are the most common formats for digital videos. The challenge in trying to pinpoint one particular format as the industry standard is that the technology that is used for content delivery evolves so quickly that it is hard to say what is dominant at any given point.

SELF-PUBLISHING

In the last decade an entirely new form of publishing has emerged: self-publishing. The widespread adoption of e-readers and the introduction of low-cost direct-to-print publication services from companies like Amazon have caused self-publishing to flourish. Historically self-publishing was reserved for wealthy individuals, universities, or organizations. Today anyone who has a computer can write and publish their work commercially for very little cost.

Some people consider this new trend a threat to the traditional publishing companies because of several factors. First, the marketplace is flooded with books written by self-publishing authors, making it harder to promote traditionally published books effectively. Second, many authors have decided to forego submitting their work to publishers and have instead gone self-published. Third, the royalty rates that authors receive when they self-publish are much higher, around 70 percent of the total book sales, whereas traditional publishing royalties are 15 to 20 percent and often paid over a much longer time frame.

The initial reception of the self-publishing movement by readers has been enthusiastic. They now have access to new authors and lower-priced books. The initial reaction of the

The power of desktop publishing software and self-publishing channels has created overnight mega-successful authors. Eighteen-year-old Abigail Gibbs earned a major book deal after self-publishing a series of vampire-themed novels.

publishing industry has been negative, mostly due to the concern that self-publishing will harm traditional publishing.

There is tremendous growth in the self-publishing realm and lots of opportunity for new kinds of jobs and services. Most of the roles that a traditional publishing company performs, including design, layout, and general editing, are also necessary for self-published titles. There are many new companies that have formed with the goal of providing services to authors who self-publish. Anyone who is interested in a career in publishing may want to explore options within the self-publishing arena. The skills required are similar to those needed to work in traditional publishing but also include an entrepreneurial spirit and the ability to do many different kinds of jobs all at once.

THE FUTURE

Just what does the future of publishing look like? That is open to debate. There will surely be much more growth in e-book and self-publishing. There will be a big change in the way that publishers search for new authors, including by scouring the many authors who self-publish.

There will certainly be ample career opportunities in publishing during the next decade, especially for those who have strong computer skills and have invested in their education in the form of college and other advanced degrees. There will also certainly be big changes in the kinds of jobs available at publishers, and any employee who is willing to embrace new technologies, new methods, and new approaches will be rewarded with ever greater responsibility and opportunity.

CMS (Content management system) A database-driven application that efficiently organizes content so that it can be easily stored, discovered, and retrieved.

copyright The legal protection that prevents theft of artistic content and is administered by the U.S. Copyright Office.

desktop publishing software Software used to enable the creation, editing, and design of printed or digital published content.

DRM (Digital rights management) A concept and method for protecting intellectual property when it is in a digital format.

EPUB A file format used by many e-readers, tablets, and desktop applications for the display of published content.

freelancer Someone who does work for many different companies as an independent outside worker.

literary agent A professional who helps authors find publishers for the author's work.

metadata Data that describes the attributes of data. Photos, text, and finished publications are all described by metadata, such as author, photographer, date, and more.

profit and loss (P&L) A summary found by adding all the costs of a project with all the income from a project.

project management software Software used to improve the management of projects from start to finish. The software helps keep projects on track for a successful and on-time completion.

spreadsheet A computer application that allows for the manipulation and analysis of data.

word processor A software application that allows for the creation of written content.

XML (Extensible markup language) XML is a programming language that allows content to be easily created, edited, and displayed across a wide variety of formats.

Association of American Publishers (AAP)
455 Massachusetts Avenue NW, Suite 700
Washington, DC 20001-2777
(212) 255-0200
Web site: http://www.publishers.org
The AAP is a trade association focused on advocating the
    issues and goals of the publishing industry to both gov-
    ernment and industry. The membership is comprised
    of many publishing companies from across the United
    States and across many fields of publishing.

The Association of Canadian Publishers (ACP)
174 Spadina Avenue, Suite 306
Toronto, ON M5T 2C2
Canada
(416) 487-6116
Web site: http://www.publishers.ca
The ACP is an industry association focused on assisting
    its members to maintain a strong and vibrant publish-
    ing industry in Canada. Members of the ACP are all
    Canadian-based and owned publishers.

Copyright Alliance
1224 M Street NW
Suite 101
Washington, DC 20005
(202)540-2243
Web site: http://www.copyrightalliance.org

The Copyright Alliance is a nonprofit educational and
public interest organization focused on all issues related
to copyright and its impact on artists and professionals in
the publishing world.

International Digital Publishing Forum (IDPF)
93 S. Jackson St. #70719
Seattle, WA 98104
(206)451-7250
Web site: http://idpf.org
The IDPF is the body responsible for maintaining the EPUB
format and maintains a forum to foster the discussion
about the ongoing changes in the publishing world.

The Journal of Electronic Publishing (JEP)
Michigan University Library
913 S. University Avenue
Ann Arbor, MI 48109-1190
Web site: http://www.journalofelectronicpublishing.org
The JEP is a forum focused on discussion and research in
the fields of electronic publishing.

WEB SITES

Due to the changing nature of Internet links, Rosen Publishing
has developed an online list of Web sites related to the subject
of this book. This site is updated regularly. Please use this link
to access the list:

http://www.rosenlinks.com/CICT/ePub

Anderson, Jeff. *Everyday Editing*. Portland, ME: Stenhouse Publishers, 2007.

Eckstut, Arielle, and David Henry Sterry. *The Essential Guide to Getting Your Book Published: How to Write It, Sell It, and Market It . . . Successfully*. New York, NY: Workman Publishing, 2010.

Embree, Mary. *Starting Your Career as a Freelance Editor: A Guide to Working with Authors, Books, Newsletters, Magazines, Websites, and More*. New York, NY: Allworth Press, 2012.

Hauschildt, Sofia. *CMS Made Simple 1.6: Beginners Guide*. Birmingham, England: Packt Publishers, 2010.

Lee, Marshall. *Bookmaking: Editing, Design, Production*. 3rd ed. New York, NY: W.W. Norton & Company, 2009.

Levine, Mark. *The Fine Print of Self-Publishing: Everything You Need to Know About the Costs, Contracts, and Process of Self-Publishing*. 4th ed. Minneapolis, MN: Bascom Hill Publishing Group, 2011.

Miller, Steve J., and Cherie K Miller. *Sell More Books!: Book Marketing and Publishing for Low Profile and Debut Authors Rethinking Book Publicity After the Digital Revolutions*. Acworth, GA: Wisdom Creek Press, 2011.

Navasky, Victor S. *The Art of Making Magazines: On Being an Editor and Other Views from the Industry* (*Columbia Journalism Review* Books). New York, NY: Columbia University Press, 2012.

Norton, Scott. *Developmental Editing: A Handbook for Freelancers, Authors, and Publishers* (Chicago Guides toWriting, Editing, and Publishing). Chicago, IL: University of Chicago Press, 2009.

Saller, Carol Fisher. *The Subversive Copy Editor: Advice from Chicago (or, How to Negotiate Good Relationships with Your Writers, Your Colleagues, and Yourself)*. Chicago, IL: University of Chicago Press, 2009.

Sambuchino, Chuck. *2013 Guide to Literary Agents*. Cincinnati, OH: Writer's Digest Books, 2012.

Smith, Kelvin. *The Publishing Business: From p-books to ebooks*. London, England: AVA Publishing, 2012.

Underdown, Harold D. *The Complete Idiot's Guide to Publishing Children's Books*. 3rd ed. New York, NY: Alpha Books, 2008.

Balkwill, Richard, and Gill Davies. *The Professionals'
    Guide to Publishing: A Practical Introduction to
    Working in the Publishing Industry.* Philadelphia, PA:
    Kogan Page Limited, 2011.
Baverstock, Alison. *How to Get a Job in Publishing.* London,
    England: A & C Black, 2008.
Clark, Giles, and Angus Phillips. *Inside Book Publishing.* New
    York, NY: Routledge, 2008.
Eberts, Marjorie. *Careers for Bookworms and Other Literary
    Types.* 4th ed. New York, NY: McGraw Hill, 2008.
Eggleston, Merilee, and K.D. Sullivan. *The McGraw-Hill Desk
    Reference for Editors, Writers, and Proofreaders.* New York, NY:
    McGraw-Hill, 2006.
Epstein, Jason. *Book Business: Publishing Past, Present and
    Future.* New York, NY: W.W. Norton & Company Inc., 2012.
Kampmann, Eric. *The Book Publisher's Handbook: The Seven
    Keys to Publishing Success with Six Case Studies.* New York,
    NY: Beaufort Books, 2007.
Thompson, John B. *Merchants of Culture: The Publishing Business
    in the Twenty-First Century.* New York, NY: Plume, 2012.
Woll, Thomas. *Publishing for Profit: Successful Bottom-Line
    Management for Book Publishers.* Chicago, IL: Chicago
    Review Press, 2010.
Yager, Fred, and Jan Yager. *Career Opportunities in the Publishing
    Industry.* New York, NY. Checkmark Books, 2009.

Index

ABOUT THE AUTHOR

Peter Ryan is a graduate of Villanova University and Rensselaer Polytechnic Institute. He is currently employed by a successful literary agency focused on children's and young adult books. Previously, Peter worked in the IT industry and the video game industry, where he learned firsthand how to work with content management systems and where he worked on large-scale publishing projects across multiple platforms.

PHOTO CREDITS

Cover (background), p. 1 © iStockphoto.com/Andrey Prokhorov; front cover (inset) © iStockphoto.com/Alexey Tkachenko; pp. 4–5 Till Jacket/Photononstop/Getty Images; p. 8 iStockphoto/Thinkstock; pp. 10–11 © Bill Aron/PhotoEdit; p. 14 Image Source/Getty Images; pp. 17, 66 Bloomberg/Getty Images; p. 19 Screenshot of Creative Commons Choose a License Web page, CC BY 3.0; p. 22 AP Images/Barnes and Noble; p. 23 Tap Magazine/Future/Getty Images; pp. 26–27 Jupiterimages/Photos.com/Thinkstock; p. 28 Blend Images/Shutterstock.com; p. 31 Robert Daly/OJO Images/Getty Images; pp. 32–33 Pixsooz/Shutterstock.com; p. 36 © Brigette Sullivan/PhotoEdit; p. 40 Screenshot from http://en.wikipedia .org/wiki/File:Scribus-1.3-Linux.png/GPL; p. 42 Karen Huang; p. 44 Jim Watson/AFP/Getty Images; p. 47 Digital Vision/Thinkstock; p. 50 © AP Images; p. 53 Jacek Chabraszewski/Shutterstock.com; p. 56 David McNew/Getty Images; p. 59 Screenshot from http://calibre-ebook.com/demo#screenshots. Calibre Web site © Kovid Goyal; p. 60 Brendan O'Sullivan/Photolibrary/Getty Images; p. 63 © iStockphoto. com/franckreporter; p. 69 Rex Feature via AP Images; interior page border image © iStockphoto.com/Daniel Brunner; pp. 13, 20, 30, 38, 45, 48, 54, 59, 67 (text box background) © iStockphoto.com/Nicholas Belton.

Designer: Les Kanturek; Editor: Nicholas Croce;
Photo Researcher: Karen Huang